Praise for
My Appalachian Mountain Laurels

"Teresa Stutso Jewell has always proudly proclaimed herself an Appalachian poet. After reading sections of her new book, I must concur with her self-assessment. She is the real deal, a bona fide West Virginia local colorist, as well as an insightful autobiographical poet. But don't expect mindless local jingoism from Teresa. The poetry evinces a genuine love-hate relationship with her region of origin—love for the riches of the land, the food, the people, as depicted in 'And You Think We're Poor?', which deconstructs the usual, simplistic dichotomies of poverty and wealth. And the hatred—the destruction of that land and those condemned to the mines by coal mining conglomerates: 'Coal dust resting on our windows/Can't raise them up when the wind blows...' Ultimately, however, Teresa's poetry transcends the evils of coal and even depicts a narrator who runs 'away from this/and [finds] I have been running in circles.' In the end, triumphantly, the narrator of 'I Am From...' accepts her station: 'I am where I'm from.' These poems are rich in sensuous detail of place, food, and culture. A part of that culture, religion, resounds epically and Biblically in the majestic (I almost wrote 'holy') rhetoric of 'The Last Supper in Appalachia.' Wow, what a poem! Read for yourself and both weep and rejoice at once."

—**Louis Gallo,** Recipient of NEA award for fiction; founding editor and publisher of the now inactive journals *Barataria Review* and *Books: A New Orleans Review*; author of the forthcoming volumes of poetry: *Crash and Clearing the Attic, Archaeology*. Chapbooks include *The Ten Most Important Questions of the Twentieth Century, The Abomination of Fascination, Status Updates,* and *The Truth Changes*

"Teresa Jewell's new collection is a hymn sung to mountains, memories, and all the rugged beauty and challenge of life in the West Virginia hills. In her poem 'Things That Make My Simple Soul Glad,' we are reminded of daily joys, such as 'camping near a stream, good lemonade, and talking with God.' Readers can savor all of life's goodness and possibility in Jewell's 'poetry from the heart and not the mind.'"

—**Rita Quillen,** Author of *Hiding Ezra* and *Wayland*

"Through beautiful poetry, Teresa Jewell gives a glimpse of life growing up in an Appalachian mining town in West Virginia. The author enlightens the reader to the fun and love of a small community. The mines provided for the families while leaving memories of happiness, and some of sadness."

—**Elizabeth Hardin Buttke,** Author of *Deep in the Holler: Appalachian Tales* and *Tell Me a Story: Appalachian Tales*

My Appalachian Mountain Laurels

Teresa Stutso Jewell

Jan-Carol Publishing, Inc
"every story needs a book"

My Appalachian Mountain Laurels
Teresa Stutso Jewell
Published October 2019
Little Creek Books
Imprint of Jan-Carol Publishing, Inc
All rights reserved
Copyright © 2019 by Teresa Stutso Jewell
Illustrations by Teresa Stutso Jewell

This is a work of fiction. Any resemblance to actual persons, either living or dead is entirely coincidental. All names, characters and events are the product of the author's imagination.

This book may not be reproduced in whole or part, in any manner whatsoever without written permission, with the exception of brief quotations within book reviews or articles.

ISBN: 978-1-950895-21-2
Library of Congress Control Number: 2019952946.

You may contact the publisher:
Jan-Carol Publishing, Inc
PO Box 701
Johnson City, TN 37605
publisher@jancarolpublishing.com
jancarolpublishing.com

I dedicate this book to another mountain poet, Geneve Sparks, who shared her poems with me.

Letter to the Reader

If you are from the Appalachian Mountains, you will understand the words I write, and I hope it makes music to your ears. If you are not from our mountains, perhaps you will get a better understanding of how lovely our world can be. I hope it will open your eyes and your heart, then you too will love our mountains.

Table of Contents

Introduction: Coal Dirt 1
A West Virginia Coal Camp Dream 3
To You Coal Miner 4
The Recliner 5
Putting His Babies to Bed 6
The Old Family Cemetery 7
My Own Spot Down by the Creek 8
The Last Supper in Appalachia 10
My Daddy's Dinner Bucket 11
I Am From 12
Do Not Feel Sorry for Me 13
Changes and Remembrances 14
And You Think We're Poor? 16
A Simple Summer Rain 17
The Old Path 18

Introduction: The Nature of Things 21
Walking to the Top So I Can See 22
The Skeleton 23
The Senses of Spring 24
Ran and Sun 25
Mother Nature Needs Love 26
Morning's Gifts 27

Inspiration 28
Little Fern 29
The Plea of Brother Mountain 30
The Mermaid's Letter to Humans 32
Italia 34
The Kitchen Table 36
The Whale's Letter to Humans 38
The Morning is Mine 40
I Lost a Friend Today 44
Greening Up 46
Regina Operaia 47

Introduction: The Romantic Side of Me 49
A Wish Upon a Breeze 50
Delivering the Gift: Honoring Marilou Awiakta 51
I Am America! 52
Junctures 54
Keeper of the Art 55
Looking Through the Italian Mist 56
Ode to the Wind 57
The Sapphire Ring 58
The Truth About Art 60
The Wedding Poem 61
There Was a Time 62
What? 63
Things That Make My Simple Soul Glad 64

Introduction: Daydreams and Thinking Back 67
In the Search for Peace 68
An Ancient Meadow 70

Always Together as a Song 72
In My Dreams..73
In Just One Night..74
Is There a Question About Most Women?..77
It is She..78
Life as a Chicken Salad 79
Queen of the Egypt, Daughter of Isis 80
The Crossroads...83
Sybil by the Sea..84
The Most Torturous Night...86
'Twas the Day After Christmas 88

Introduction: My Older Days 91
What About the Word "Old"?..92
Evolution, Revolution, and Change 93
Me in the Mirror 94
At the Hour of His Death...96
Miss Ruth is Missing 97
He Died..98
My Time 100
Picky in My Old Age 101
Renewal 102
The Retirement Cabin 103
The Time Machine 104
The Puzzle of the Garden...105
Time to Think 106
My Class Reunion 107

Coal Dirt

I could not write a piece of poetry without talking about the special place I was raised. I was born smack dab in the middle of the Appalachian Mountains in a small coal town. In my early youth, War, West Virginia was a boom town. All the businesses were open and doing great. Our little town had two theaters with matinees every day and late-night movies, and if you didn't get there early, you'd have a hard time finding a seat during any of the movie times. The streets were full of shoppers, business people, young people and old people. I watched my paradise gradually wither and die during my young adult years.

My father was a coal miner and so was his father. My mom was born in the mountains as well. Coal mining was a part of my life, just as the dirty air we breathed. I was raised with other children who shared the same experience. All the adults in our town either worked in the mines or had jobs that were kindred to them. Everything depended upon the mines.

We lost a lot of good men to mining deaths and black lung. We also lost clear running streams, roads ruined by heavily laden coal trucks, and safe places to live and play. We lost the assurances and comfort of knowing your dad would come home safe after working their shift at the mines. This left a hard place in our souls while growing up there. We also lost our friends as their families had to move because some of the mines closed. The history books called this "The Great Appalachian Migration," which pulled a lot of good families apart. There wasn't a family that wasn't touched by this, in one way or the other.

Even after all the losses, the hardships, and the heartbreaks, it was a paradise to me. I did move from my little town, but not far. I could not leave the mountains, as I feared I would wither and die too, without the safety of the towering tree line that holds up the sky. Many things have changed in the mountains, but the good things have remained in my memories. When people have to leave, the economy goes with them. Hard luck is not a stranger. A new time will come with new ways. One must have faith. The deepest part of my soul is here, in Appalachia.

I do hope you enjoy my thoughts, my prayers, and my mountain heritage. It has taken a lifetime to realize how blessed I was, how blessed I am, and just how blessed I will be.

Thank you all and may you all be "Mountain Blessed."

A West Virginia Coal Camp Dream

*I was Peter Pan, Wendy, Huck Finn, and Amelia Earhart
using my imagination as my only vehicle
flying away or floating away to somewhere unknown,
the escape of my parent's coal dust covered dreams.
Not seeing skinny kids without a lunch ticket
or barefoot children when school started,
I never again wanted to hear another thing about welfare
or food stamps or cars with busted mufflers.
My dream was to be somewhere else
where my feet would be clean all day
not covered to my ankles with fine black soot.
To be far away from the snaking Norfolk & Western
screaming at the railroad crossing and never slowing down,
a place when you had a cut it would heal clean and forgotten
not in that place where a wound would heal blue
to mark us as a blue tattoo with a message.
I have been busy running away from this
and found I have been running in circles
there is not a place that doesn't have one of us in it
we carry our blue scars and nightmares of mountain bumps
where ever we go.
Hard times seem to be just as hard to lose
no matter where you land.*

To You Coal Miner

The mines that took my daddy's life and the coal mine where I gave mine,
Turned us all away today, it's closed for good this time.
What am I to do, this is all I've ever done?
I went in the dark damp hole never seeing the daylight sun,
My hard-working wife and my kids depend on me
Now it looks darker outside than inside could ever be.
I can't believe the mine closed today for good this time and left my soul in strife.
My regular payday is over. How do I tell my wife?
How can I look into her eyes? Somebody tell me how?
Guess I'll go back to farmin', fencin', and takin' up the plow,
But how will I pay for the seed that I need when I need money now?
Never thought I would be back here, now that I am in need...
And my children I must clothe and a family I must feed.
The lure of the mine and a good payday made me leave my unplowed fields,
As the payday offered was better than the farm could yield.
I thought that I had struck it rich when I went inside the mine
Then the laws came down making it harder to work as they cut back on our time
Guess that mine that took my daddy's life has given me a sign.
Farmin' and trying to make ends meet will test my very soul.
Guess I'll be buried in good bottom land and not crushed beneath the coal.

The Recliner

Dad swore they put ether in it when they put it together,
He couldn't keep his eyes open twenty minutes after sitting in it.
He would try to watch the ball game
Pull back the lever and his feet would fly up
And his body would lean back,
It seemed he stretched clean across the living room.
He would try to jump up to get a better view of the hit
And would scream and cuss when the ump would call it wrong
"Are you blind, ump?" he would shout with a raised fist and feet in the air.
Even after all the excitement, it was more than he could fight
He would snore through the last couple innings
And wonder what happened when mom would come in
To tell him it was time to go to bed.
Dazed and confused, he blamed it all on that brown, Naugahyde recliner.
We had it recovered twice.
He had scratched the wooden floors where he sat
As he pushed and rode that recliner through all the sports events.
Bread crumbs, chips, and candy wrappers seemed to gather around the radius of his chair
It was his throne of greatest authority and manhood,
No one dared to sit in dad's chair.
He eventually wore it out as did he,
I would give anything
To have him and that old recliner back.

Putting His Babies to Bed

He gets home late, tired and hungry,
Worked in the mine time and a half today.
Dinner is in the oven waiting warm for him
His family is waiting too.
Baths have been given and the reading done
Sleep will not come until daddy tucks them in.
His big hands, rough knuckles with black stained fingernails and blue scars
Tenderly cover those small bodies with their fluffy blankets,
Kisses and pats each trusting little head.
The babies feel safe and satisfied.
But it is raining and he worries
The thick forest that lived once behind the house is gone,
Timbers big and small are gone.
The land slides each time it rains.
He can't sleep tonight; he listens for the mud.
It is early spring and the loose soil thaws.
Must his family and others pay the price?
Some passers-by think it is not as pretty as it once was
Beauty is not the problem.
Mountain Top Removal is not just ugly,
It is a danger to us all.
Can you sleep tonight?

The Old Family Cemetery

Gather your young'uns about you
tell them the history of your clan.
Tell them your mother was a lady
you father was a coal mining man
your grandpa worked on the railroad
grandma made sweet apple pies
and in this family cemetery
history of the clan here testifies.
There, buried is a rebel soldier
another uncle died in Vietnam
a maiden aunt, who was a teacher
she lived alone but taught most all of them.
Great-uncle John was a farmer
he cleared almost all this land around
he raised thirteen children on this farmland
and gave the clan this sacred patch of ground.
The first one buried was old Ruarc
he came from Ireland across the sea
he left his family and his country
to make a life, part of our history.
Family blood is something to believe in
and protect no matter what the cost
without the strong tether of blood kin
your roots will wither and be lost.
There may be a doctor or a preacher,
a roust-about or just a raggedy man
no matter what they did for a living
always be family proud of them.

My Own Spot Down by the Creek

There used to be a special spot on the rocks
down by the creek, where I rested my fishing pole
and my rusty can of worms,
cut out of the stone
for me and my stuff.
Rocks so smooth and weather worn
carved long ago by some raging torrent
or maybe by the Hand of God;
trout loved to tease me there
as they slid through the cool, busy water
fractured light reflected their shiny scales
along the brilliant rocky bottom
with the mica sparkling like a spilled treasure
changing colors that mirror the sky.
I did more daydreaming in those days
assuming it would always stay the same, waiting for my return;
I did return one day to that sleepy little hollow
with its quick singing stream
to find it gone. The road was barely there,
the hollow had been filled in with rocks and rubble
and the mountain was gone.

My little creek vanished along with her birds and fish
my large stones were gone,
so was everything else.
There was a sign that hung on a large gate
that stretched across the road,
No Trespassing
By order of the Black Diamond Creek Coal Company
So, I turned the car around
and took my little boy home.

The Last Supper in Appalachia

"This is my body which has been given to you
take this in remembrance of Me."
The mountain stood and the man
took the mountain given by God,
and he did eat.
He then passed the cup and said,
"This is my blood, drink this in remembrance of Me,"
and the man dammed the waters and polluted it
for the sake of prosperity.
He said, *"For whenever you eat this bread*
and drink this cup, you proclaim..."
and reclaim, remove and forget,
and when the Lord comes
there will be no beautiful gifts
for they will be gone,
as pearls thrown before the swine.
Father forgive them their trespasses
and their evictions and their murders,
bless the faithful who remain faithful
looking toward heaven
into brown clouded sickening air
and the rains come to wash the earth away.
For the people and the forests
have been sacrificed
as the Lamb

My Daddy's Dinner Bucket

Watching Daddy walk down the road to catch his ride
the dinner bucket swings with his manly gate,
a silver cylinder with a black handle
with special compartments for two sandwiches, a banana, and water.
Daddy went into the mines every day with his bucket
inside a lunch packed by loving hands,
scrubbed everyday,
filled with magical cakes
from the store he passed on his way home.
The bucket rests on the kitchen table in the mornings
the sign that he made it home safely
sleeping in his bed as we quietly leave for school.
If his bucket stayed on the table for a while
a sign hard times had found us,
strikes happened often.
I remember when the time came
when he no longer left for the mine,
he went there every day in his dreams.
I wish I knew where that old silver bucket is now
filled with dark, soot-stained
beat up coal camp memories.

I Am From...

I am from the mountains of tall pines
From collard greens to bright moonshine
From casks full of dark Italian wine
And cut cabbage set in the brine

I am from a family saying grace
China, silver, and tablecloth of lace
Where black damp waits without a trace
Existing at a different pace

I am from the deep, dark hollow
The midday sun the rest in shadows
Coal dust resting on our windows
Can't raise them up when the wind blows

Praising God and coal miner songs
Churches and unions, we all belong
Lingering on either not for long
Be it right or be it wrong
I am where I'm from.

Do Not Feel Sorry for Me,
(because I am from the mountains)

Do not look at me with that pitiful, sympathetic glaze

You look down at me with a quiet disgust.

You think that I am lower and unworthy of your attention?

I am from right here, right under your nose

I am educated, I am clean, I have common sense

I am from another social class. Thank God!

I do not race around in a maze trying to get from one place to another.

You think I am common

I have many things you do not have.

My friends and family are hardworking people.

Our people are church-going people, and honorable.

A handshake and our word is our bond.

We do not need a lawyer or a court to secure private matters

We know how to act in public, we are modest.

We do not flaunt wealth, or our feelings of love or passion in public.

Money is important to us,

but I have done without it before

Having money is not as important

as my God, family and country.

It is you who needs the pity,

Do not feel sorry for me or my kind.

If you don't like being around us,

Try Hell, we won't be there!

Changes and Remembrances

New land, strange people, unfamiliar customs,
American language,
facing hatred and fear in the mine with whispers of union
empty promises from toothy, smiling faces and pats on the back
a shovel and pick in his hands for someone else's treasure.
Home, the place where love is, a busy place, mama and
God always there,
peppers and tomatoes on the fence, the chickens in the back
the barrels of freshly made wine, the cow and the goat,
gun over the door.
The children like stair steps have their own work,
hardly time for play
Mama baking Italian bread that smelled sweetly through
the screen door
floating through the camp, with the early morning breeze
pasta hung on drying cords in the bedrooms,
while the bread was baking.
Papa sold his wine, mama sold her bread, eggs and cheese
the boys collected cans and glass, delivered newspapers
the girls helped ladies clean house or watch their babies.

They all worked together on their own union...

one for all and all for one,

clean clothing, polished shoes, and patched mantillas for mass on Sundays.

Not the homeland of their birth,

but making this new land a place for their death

nothing regretted, they did the right thing, fed, clothed, loved, nurtured, and educated

starting new traditions, remembering the old,

entwined in their sweet success

lingering memories of those bygone days in their eyes,

and in their hearts, in our faded pictures

the portraits on the wall,

the cane leaning against the doorway,

every time we smell homemade bread, or tomato sauce simmering,

honoring our dead in a special mass

remembering the smell of one of those thin, wrinkled little cigars...

And You Think We're Poor?

We eat the beans that we grow
shucked sweet corn
slathered in fresh yellow cow butter,
cornmeal and buttermilk don't come from the store.
Pickled watermelon rind and everything else,
dandelion and sweet berry wine
sunshine, moonshine
hot, fried apple pies.
A field of potato mounds
grease killed mess'o greens and onions,
freshly killed hogs
our own beef.
Jars of apple butter and pickled beets,
no locked doors
bawling coonhounds and skittish barn cats
bobwhites calling softly from the meadow in the evening,
crows loudly breaking the silence of the morning.
Harsh mountain winter,
gentle singing spring,
clear running mountain streams
trout and deep skillet fried catfish
sitting porches and iced tea.
Talking politics at the post office
friends and family are always home
God-fearing, but fearing no man
and you think we're poor?

A Simple Summer Rain

Clouds gathering on the mountain tops, a signal to me only
a summer rain is a welcomed friend that visits sometimes
I used to love running and twirling as the droplets hit my face,
Running boldly barefooted over the slick, smooth stones
leading me to the pathway of our orchard.
My feet and toes love touching the wet cool grass
feeling the earth soften beneath my feet,
my summer clothing clinging to my body
my hair in curls and flying out as I turned in circles
dancing with the rhythm of the wind and rain.
Each tree was my partner as I danced with each one
their blossoms raining down on me as if giving me their gifts
too soon, the rain would change her mind and go somewhere else
returning home with a triumphant feeling of no fear
my mother only saw wet cloths, a wet child with muddy feet
she didn't have a clue.

The Old Path

I am walking a path that I used to walk long ago
I hadn't been here in many years
Thinking that I should go back to reminisce and so,
The memories were all gone, and it brought me to tears.

Where are the people who used to walk along this path with me?
The houses and people are all gone, where did they all go?
All those happy, friendly faces I needed and wanted to see
Thought I was the only one who left such a long time ago.

Time changed things from vibrant green to grey and brown,
The smells of beans and wood smoke are no longer in the wind.
What was once there has been abandoned or rusted to the ground
The only thing I recognize is the train tracks that snaked around the bend.

Not only did I find things changed, I found that I did too
Everybody that I knew left when they closed the mine,
Common sense told me to go, what was I to do?
I went to the city—a different place and different time.

I wish I could turn back time and resurrect the town
Before the mine took our lives and killed our memories,
Before the floods, way before our creeks turned brown,
Before food stamps, black lung, and before the coal companies

Heaven may hold the only place that I would recognize
The miners and their widows I am sure will all be there,
The big coal company owners will be cut down to size.
It's the only place where we can go,
Where people are treated fair.

The Nature of Things

My childhood was happily spent in the mountains or on the creek bank. I knew each path and rock cliff all around and behind our house. I was a blessed child as all I had to do was walk a few steps from my front door and I was in the woods. I had a short walk to the creek. Our steep mountains have deep valleys and where I lived, we had good daylight from about 9:00 am and until about 4:30 in the afternoon. A short way down was the creek in the middle, and I was not far from fun. I am sure the adults didn't find as much fun as I did. I was a free and easy child who played where I wanted to, such as swinging on grapevines, climbing trees, making cabins or playhouses, or fishing or wading when I felt like it.

I have always been a nature lover. My whole young life's happiness was because of the nature that was just outside my door. I was an observer of nature, as I learned about the seasons and the different animals of the woods. I learned about myself as well. I still find peace when I get in my car and drive into the countryside, away from the major highways. If there is a country road within a hundred miles, you can bet my husband and I have traveled it with great pleasure.

I write to soothe my soul while I remember my joyous times as a child. I want to share this wonderful peace that is such a gift to all of us. Go find your place of peace.

Walking to the Top So I Can See

I love walking up to the mountain top
to see through the veil of early morning mist
looking past the laurel and vine
the sun will kiss the mountain lips first,
the deep breath vision of valleys and the rivers
sensing the damp essence of the pine
the hawk is calling to his mate.
The ancient ones still visit,
doe and fawn have lain here
as this spot holds their warmth where they slept
a peaceable place
the fox lingers in the shadows watching.
Down below there are many shadows
the people below have forgotten how to cleanse their souls
ridding themselves of the earth's parasites
I have found my cleanser and my stress reliever
Here, above all that.

The Skeleton

Down the road, I've passed it many times,
a lone chimney upon a hill, peeping through the tall grass.
Today I stopped and climbed the hill to see
I slowly waded through the tall, independent grass and creeper vines
there on that knoll, a fireplace and chimney standing, remembering
the crumbling, blackened stone foundation was a testimony
charred, scattered, rotting logs were there as a witness
this had been a home, a sanctuary for someone.

I walked through the remains carefully as not to disturb this peace
the fireplace was the heart of this home
Now, the chimney supports a vine where lizards visit
through sickness, health, laughter and tears, darkness and light
those who came through its doors are gone now.

I felt as if I were visiting an unkept grave of a forgotten loved one
requiem came to me as I stood there quietly
the lone wind whistled through the loose stones
the usefulness of its being is over
it rests, waiting for time to take it all
no names or headstones there to remember,
just that old chimney
standing through the ages
in the thick uncut grass.

The Senses of Spring

Can you smell spring? I can.

It smells green, a scent of trees awakening

The ground smells of moist earth

The slickness after the thaw

The sweetness of forgotten leaves that fell in the fall.

Maybe it is just that scent of new life that thrills me

Preparing the ritual for all to see,

I can hear the little frogs, the peepers sing

I can feel the breezes from the south that excite every living thing

I can finally feel the winds changing, nature sings of her survival

All my senses are more aware, and alert to herald springs arrival.

Rain and Sun

I've gotten used to rain in my life
It rained the day I was born
I've had my share of worries and strife.
My heart is battered and worn
I've had my share of happiness
I guess the balance is even,
Rains one day and shines the next
Thankful I am still breathin'.
I've gotten used to the rain in my life
But the sunshine was there too
It's how fate rolled the dice
What was I supposed to do?
We have to take the bitter with the sweet
It's our oasis in the desert
We have to look for the best of life
It doesn't take that much of an effort.
And we must keep on...

Mother Nature Needs Love

I am the forest
I am the river
You can come and talk to me
I will listen.
I am the wind
As well as the meadow
I am a treasure, full of wonder
Come discover me for yourself.
Do you love me?
Do you honor me?
Tell the stories of my beauty to your young
So they will love me too.

Morning's Gifts

Morning,
forced intrusion of amber light
announced by feathered criers
moving trees in its wake,
wanting to be stronger than
his sister, Evening.
Awaken, can you not see
the gifts of Morning?
Treasures of dew and pastel orchid sky
leaving sapphire glistening
sparkling emerald shards of grass
missed by late risers and dry landers.
Fishermen pay homage,
pulling up their laden nets
snares of silver and gold
from the awakening ocean
appearing like crumpled aluminum foil
gulls, frigates, pipers calling
already at work.
Behold, the rising sun.

Inspiration

The book I read and read again
the music I heard in my dreams
the vibrato of a crimson sunset
the feel of sheer, iridescent fabric
my feelings upon any given day
words of encouragement
the ambiance of an older restaurant
the crisp green of a spring salad
the curling steam from a hot cup of coffee
the smiling face of a sun-kissed child
the tears of a life-weary old woman
the hopelessness of an invisible homeless person
the sincere-ness of a needful prayer
loved or forsaken
the peace of alone
amber morning through my eyelids
soft woven evening
stiff, cool white sheets and crisp pillowcases
candlelight is reflecting thoughts...
The poem is written.

Little Fern

Sister winter had her time
to run among the hills,
Now it's time for spring to wake
and hear the spring bird's trill.
The little fern lies sleeping
'neath the acorns and the leaves,
as slowly he awakens, the sky he longs to see.
"Arise oh young and face the sun,
for spring is here and winter's done,"
he hears Mother Nature call
and pushes back the covers,
and stands up straight and tall.

The Plea of Brother Mountain

I Am a Mountain.
I have lived through many years alongside my other brothers
I was here to watch the first two-legged red children roam through my hills and valleys.
They were the first beings who honored me,
I spoke to them and they listened and learned
They walked softly upon my back
Every step taken was careful not to bruise.
I fed them and sheltered them
I guided the waters that fell upon my head
Down to where they drank,
They did not take anything that was not given with love.
The red children lived many years within my shadow in peace
Sadly, as I have watched the eons come and go
So did my red children.

They have been replaced by others who are takers
They have plowed my valleys
Burned and scorched me
Took my ancient timber
Tunneled inside into my black rich veins.
Even now there are some of them buried inside me
They seek the riches that make me poor
They care not for the sacred reason I am here
They have carved a highway deep into my sides.
I cannot see my brothers
Where are they?
Where are my red children?
Please come back to save me.

The Mermaid's Letter to Humans

To Whom It May Concern:

All the oceans are my home. My world is a place of sweet movement and broken light.

The current of the water is like the wind on dry land, and the schools of fish move like your birds on the wing.

Our worlds are alike yet so very different.

I cannot breathe your air, you cannot breathe my water

I cannot walk on your land, but I do not want to.

And you cannot glide through my waters as I do.

You try to imitate us, but you look clumsy with your water dance.

Our movements are graceful like the kelp forests in the current

Our music is the song of whales and porpoises.

We do not welcome your intrusion into our world, we never did.

Once we lured you onto the reefs where your wooden vessels crumbled.

We stopped that game as it was too easy and boring. You never learned.

You come back again and again to destroy our beautiful world.

Your black oil chokes my family and makes the water strange.

Your machines pound our world and cloud our water,

Your careless fishing leaves the waters bloody as you have left your world.

Must you destroy all that you know?

Perhaps we will return to the old ways, with our anger, lure you to the reef,

Summon large waves to cover your land and your families.

Perhaps we will reclaim the land that we so unselfishly entrusted you to honor.

We will not die so kindly. Take care humans.

Sincerely.

Italia

My first footprint upon Italian soil

felt different than the earth I tread upon yesterday

yet so strangely familiar as I gaze upon

soft little houses so close together

placed on the lap of ancient mountains

like beautiful wildflowers.

Colorful mosses bathing in the western sun

clotheslines full of white shirts and table cloths

cobblestone streets talking as your sandals press against them

statues frozen in a moment of stilled history

from a more beautiful era and eye

God visiting, talking among the red-robed cardinals

walking soldiers and the black and white-frocked sisters.

Pigeons fly in unison like a magnificent choreographed presentation

around the large piazzas and fountains on an invisible current

as tourists throw pieces of bread to lure

them from their dance and to their cameras.

Focus on everything quickly before

the changes in sunset and time

where tempered evening smells of sweetbreads, herbs, and wine

as the perfume rises mixing with the street's visions

of lovers and loners as they too

dance a beautiful ballet of fantasies of time

the music of fear of being alone is so

strange and unfamiliar to those who stay.

The Kitchen Table

My grandmother gave the old oak table to mom when she got a new one

mom used it all those years

wonderful meals served to family and friends

on that rectangle center of our universe, the hub to the wheel.

Homework, Christmas cards signed, sympathy cards placed in purple envelopes

checks written, bills paid, presents wrapped, stories told, company served, birthday cakes,

funeral arrangements, tears, coffee cup rings, burns, Kool-Aid stains and Bible readings,

first baths and first aid, Girl Scout cookie orders, report cards signed with a heavy hand

dough rolled, fruit canned, everyday plates, cereal bowls and a turkey platter,

family sitting all around with held hands in simple prayer.

The table passed down again to me

I did all the same except a few extras

arts and crafts, music and poetry written

Grading papers, folded towels and groceries in plastic bags, polish and wax.

Do I need a new table?

No, I haven't the time to break a new one in

it would take eighty years to complete and catch up

the memories are embedded into every little scratch and ding

this table holds more than my family can afford

it will just have to do.

The Whale's Letter to Humans

To Whom It May Concern:

When first we appeared, we thought our world was limited and filled with strange creatures, so we grew our land legs and walked on dry soil.

We soon found it was as hostile a place as the one we left and chose to let go of our legs and regain our fins and go back to our waters. It was the right decision. We soon ruled the waters, and all knew us as royalty.

We lived in peace for thousands of years until man found us. He killed us for the fat to burn light, so he could defy the dark.

Finally, some of the humans defended us and with the few of us that were left, we began to grow and increase our numbers. We are still hunted, but that is the sacrifice we must make for our greatness and intellect.

Humans, you have a great brain. Please use it for the betterment of our earth and waters. All our time is limited, so please make the best of it. We are.

We will not harm you, we are brothers.

We will sing for you and lead you to a better life if you will just observe.

We have gone through almost extinction and changed a lot through the years, yet here we are strong and beautiful.

Our lives along with our little brothers and sisters depend on how you treat your world. Be a kinder species, be a learned species, be a protective species, as we have been all along.

Thank you for your immediate consideration in this matter.

Sincerely,

The Whales of the Oceans.

The Morning is Mine

5:30 in the morning

I cannot go back to sleep

the outside business will not let me

an eastern glow on my tent wall

paints long leafy shadows as they slowly move

noisy morning birds make their announcements

my husband is still sleeping

fetal position on his left side

safe in his sleeping bag

replicates an emerging insect

from its warm cocoon

his snoring is louder than the birds

We drove from the city yesterday evening

to this wilderness utopia we have known for years

we race to make camp before the sunlight dies

I fed and chained our dog

built the campfire in the center

surrounded by creek rocks and bedded in sand

moved our lawn chairs closer to catch the ambiance

our favorite radio station played memories

the warmth of the fire hypnotized and relaxed our bodies

as the fire bent its weary head
we crawled into our little tent
too tired for love, we fluffed our pillows
sleep came without encouragement or aids
the night invited my senses
perfume of pine and sweet grass
sounds of night creatures buzzing
the soft melody of the stream
the taste of dew in the air
the silk feel of our warm thick sleeping bags
the slight glow of the dying embers
compete with the crowded stars
we both slept heavy without dreams
I am pleased to be first to awaken
into a private place
this time is for me only.
I prepared the camp kitchen
rekindled the campfire with fresh wood
freed my dog and fed her
made the coffee and pulled up a chair.
why does coffee taste so much better here?
I sat back and put my feet up on the multipurpose cooler
dissecting the fractured darkness
with the easement of the gold metallic sunrise,

I relaxed and waited for the sun
to take away the damp and pea soup morning fog.
From my hot mug, rolling spiral ribbons of steam fill my nose
Young frogs and some night birds were singing their farewells
as the creatures of the light herald the morning.
I motioned to my dog to follow me and she quickly obeyed
She ran in front of me to show the way and to secure my path
I took my large "carry all" through the grass down to the stream
The stream is female I thought, a crystal rivulet, full of new life
meandering freely through the receptive terrain
willows and reeds dance and sway to her seductive music
I could not resist her call to bathe in her waters and her glory
the large rocks carved out long ago
have perfect niches for my soap and shampoo
and a warm resting place for my dog
the little birch tree volunteers to hold my towel
finding a shallow little cove, I wade out to my knees
using a big plastic cup I pour the water over my head
too cold for complete submersion this early
the water awakens every pore of my being
the cold trickle of soapy water travels down my back and my front
my skin turns to goose flesh
washing is done quickly with the aid of my dipper
the towel is a most welcomed accessory as it wraps me in a hug

rising on his set pattern, Sol spreads out his arms as he reaches for mid sky

his early warmth touches my skin gently

dressing a little faster than I did yesterday

I stepped up to the large rock and welcomed this morning

I let my hair loose to dry in his heat

along in my tote I carried fishing gear

pulling it out amidst the bottle of shampoo and soap

I found my favorite silver green lure

attached it to my line

stood up and surveyed my position

the reeds across the stream held nervous insects

and tree limbs hung low as if to tease the water with their leaves

the sun had not completely found that spot yet

I cast my line into the air

like a spiders silk it glistened as it slid into the Saffire world

the "kerplunk" sound of my lure hitting the perfect spot

quicksilver hypnotic movements find the interest of a trout

he, along with five of his rainbow brothers

surrendered themselves to me within the hour

There will be trout for breakfast this morning

my husband still sleeps

the coffee steams as I fry up my catch

I claim it all

this morning is mine. Yes!

I Lost a Friend Today

I lost a friend today
she died gasping for her last breath
coughing up brown exploding pudding
filling the room with the smell of rot,
damn those cigarettes.
She was warned but would not listen
she said she could quit anytime she wanted to
she said she enjoyed smoking
they relaxed her and finished her meal,
besides she smoked the skinny ones that were safe.
She cried when they told her she was dying
wiping her tears with orange stained fingers,
then she lit one up as soon as she walked outside.
Her house smelled of the fowl brown exhaust
her skin wrinkled and thin as used tissue paper
her curly red hair grayed early before it fell out,
she wept when her last curl was left on the pillow.

She smoked to calm her nerves,
she was hooked up to machines
tubes that let her diseased lungs drain
tubes through her nose to her stomach
a port at the base of her neck that oozed
morphine drip that didn't drip fast enough.
Her grandchildren will never know her,
never again to read a bedtime story
life will go on without her
a life cut short...gone...up in smoke.

Greening Up

Sshhh! Listen!
Do you hear them?
The little peepers
heralding the coming time.
Yes, it might snow tomorrow
but Spring, brave as she is,
has stepped into the wind
right on time!

Regina Operaia

Her pox-marked face
peeps before she slides
over the mountain.
Her majesty's full face is only visible
once a month
like clockwork.
She changes her mind
every seven days.
La Lune is the queen of the night
she rules the tides
and the seasons
ova wait patiently
for her audience
reigning over all nature.
She does not live
within her own sovereignty,
she rules from outside
so near yet so far away
she must have known
the ruin of her charge
she is safe so far.

The Romantic Side of Me

The Romantic Side of Me, isn't lovey-dovey or mushy at all. Some of my writing here, tapped into the feminine side of me and the child as well. I always wanted to be a traveler and be inspiring to anyone who would listen. I think that is why I loved to draw and paint, as it allowed me to escape into the paper of whimsical figures and places and to make my wishes visible. Later, I found literature that made my mind travel freely through all the pages I have read. Now it's my turn to place in poetry form my whimsical, dreamlike thoughts to please myself and hopefully, you the reader.

I think being half Italian and the other half split between the Scots and the Irish, I have a strange imagination. Yes, I know what you are thinking, "dang, what a combination." But this allowed me to be a "listener" to folktales and family stories as well as others' dreams and experiences. I have experienced life, love, loss, and nature, and have loved every moment of it all. See if you can find me in the poems that I write. If you are not a lover of something, I feel for you. Try a little harder to love these gifts that are before you.

A Wish Upon a Breeze

I sent a wish upon a passing breeze,
I have wished upon many things before.
This breeze was warm, quick, and took me unaware
it must have been a particular breeze
as it made me remember my time with you,
making me wish
as it travels swiftly to where you are
you will feel it pass across your lips and eyelashes,
perhaps your heart will stir
as your thoughts go back to the time of me
and you will wish upon the same breeze
while I stand here waiting for it to return.

Delivering the Gift: Honoring Marilou Awiakta

She was born to deliver a special gift

she learned from the elders of both bloods,

Corn Mother, Grandmother, and Mother Earth,

the voices of Selu and her mother asked

"What will you do for your people?"

Her soul answered, "I will write and tell the truth, for I have learned much."

History, equality, and fairness

both bloods of mountain folk and Cherokee

blended to bring the past to the present, and into the future

making strong medicine with her words,

stump setting with the Atom

listening to the sounds of the earth

teaching what she hears, she knows, and what she thinks.

I Am America!

I have been called a beautiful lady. I am known the worldwide.
I have many lovers that come for protection that cling to my side.

My skin of many colors is a mixing pot of ebony, bronze, silver, and gold,

the most desirable of skin, for we are strong, brave, and bold.

I am the mother of many children and I care for others too

They huddle close; I protect and guard them, that is what good mothers do.

I am AMERICA!

Everyone knows my name; for Thee I Sing!

I am the symbol of good, Let Freedom Ring!

Sweet land of liberty, that did not come free

To protect the life that we have now

The best for you and me,

I am AMERICA!

My profile is the seashore, too lovely to define

my strands of hair are highways which flow like the wind

flowing from east to west, north to south it seems there is no end

My eyes are the rivers, lakes, and streams that glisten aqua blue,

My heart is the Mississippi that pumps my heart blood through.

My arms hold the home hearths where my children thrive

They work, they play and pray, glad that they're alive

Other symbols and statues compare themselves to me,

They are only little specks, I am from sea to shining sea.

Their statues crumble, they are pale as weathered clay

My statue holds the torch on high, so others can see the way,

I am AMERICA!

The mother of many, the keeper of the light

I represent the strong, the free, the courageous; I am the writer of right.

Yes, I am a beautiful lady. Honor me, cherish me, be true to me, protect my honor

I am worth the sacrifice! I am worth fighting for! My warriors bear my armor.

I am AMERICA!

You get your strength from me

For I was forged from blood and bitter tears and victory.

I will never grow old or fade away in some obscurity,

My warriors will always be ready to serve and protect you and me

I will stand by you as you grow old, I am your security,

I am AMERICA!

Junctures

Your poems are not so much different than mine
our needs are different and so is our hunger
you are looking for that great adventure
in search of your first taste of fulfillment.
I have already had a few meals upon it
your colorful deep meaning metaphors
are necessary for you right now
I have been there, done that
didn't even get a T-shirt.
You must do it all
express it all
taste it all,
when you are full
one clear day
you will think of me
and realize
I was OK
after all.

Keeper of the Art

*When God created the earth
it was a work of art from pure love.
He wove the grasses into many colors,
shaped the trees to reach upward
with his mighty finger,
He dug out the loose dirt for the river flow
made the earth soft ground and cool sand,
made the animals from a single thought
being His most beautiful creative work.
He then created man as the keeper of all his art.
Man has gotten lazy and complacent at his job
the keeper does not care the way the Artist does.*

Looking Through the Italian Mist

I remember my grandfather's eyes
after all those years, still looked
like those of a visitor
never adjusting to his new sights.
My father's eyes had the same look
yet he was satisfied with what he saw.
I am a third-generation Italian
told I had a faraway mist in my eyes,
although I was born here
I long to see the things they saw,
that place in the mist with the rolling vineyards
the blue waters pushing gondolas
Foggia, Perugia, Rome, Palermo
my blood still flowing there
that I have missed and now long to find
My vision must be satisfied, as well as my soul
I pray I do not die before seeing through the mist.

Ode to the Wind

You have flipped up my gossamer skirts

Unloosed my fashionable coifed tresses

Blown the cluttered decaying leaves

Along with crumpled love notes to other places.

The trees are shaken to relieve the last year's labors,

You carry scented messages to every wild thing

As easily as you carry my kite or my balloon,

A clothesline with sheets slapping time in the wind

The ravaging hungry fires travel swiftly with you

And the squelching rain that you bring is an offering of forgiveness.

Friend and Foe

Twisting your mighty finger to stir destruction

Or pushing us along the silver water with full blossomed sails,

I respect you and long to hear your song

in my chimes hanging outside my open door.

The Sapphire Ring

"Here," he said, "I bought you a Sapphire ring to wear."
"Well," I said, "I will wear the golden ring so fair,
But I'll not belong to anyone
For I am young and just begun.
I will wear the golden ring of sapphire blue,
But I will wear it for me, and not for you."

Our love is fresh and new as early spring
But I won't be bound by a sapphire ring
I will sing your song and walk with you
But only for a while, for I have much to do.

"Here," he said, "I have a home for you."
"No," I said, "I have my own work to do
I'll live alone for the rest of my life
Living for myself and I'll be no man's wife."

I've watched my sisters with faces so fair,
marry a man with heavy burdens to bear,
grow old and wither like grapes on a vine
lose the beauty and their souls before it was time.

A promise of a golden sapphire ring
A girl thinks of the happiness his world will bring
But I have seen the trials of long-suffering
Brought on by the luster of a sapphire ring.

The Truth About Art

What is art anyway?
An expression of an emotion
that another person can visualize,
a sublime vision of either
anger, love, or nothingness
people gasp and awe at the brush stroke
the use of color, passion, or light
criticized and oversized,
the who's who must concur.
A simple caveman's hunt
painted on a wall of a cave
in Lascaux France
so pure, so perfect
hunger—famine
plenty—feast
magic—religion
a serious story portrayed in pigmented clay,
salons in Paris did not even consider
their worth as Paul Cézanne, Toulouse-Lautrec
Renoir and Daumier took their bows
to work that was not real.
Picasso wanted to be different,
to be considered a genius,
but this one simple inspired artist
alone in a cave creating by torchlight...

The Wedding Poem

*The universe has been waiting,
two hands two hearts
two become one,
two loves, one love
two people destined
joined to make stronger.
The universe already knows
that few will share this kind of love
the bond so strong, so blessed
will bear witness, an example
of how devotion was meant to be.
They breathe the same air
as he breathes in, his heart
says "I will love you forever"
When she exhales, her heart
says, "I adore you."*

There Was a Time...

They don't touch anymore

And they are comfortable with that.

They have gotten to that place where talk doesn't excite

Unless the grandchildren call, or pictures in the mail.

They barely remember that other place where they were talkers and doers

They could not keep their hands off each other when they passed.

It seemed she was always pregnant, valentines and flowers,

Their hands are by their sides not wanting to explore anymore.

Time, effort, need, want are gone.

They dress for comfort and undress to change,

Wearing comfortable shoes and driving the speed limit,

not doing anything dangerous or questionable.

They have been lucky to get this far. Safe is good.

All weather tires, first aid kits, batteries, and medical alert systems.

What?

What is it you want from me?
my soul, my heart, my blood, my future
I have agreed to give all, I promised,
but you have defaulted.
You did not sign in blood as I did
only crimson colored disappearing ink
you take up most of the bed
along with the blankets and sheets,
you tear up my bed and my dreams.
We travel these days in different circles,
My circles are smaller than yours, but mine are better structured
What? Do you want more?
you know, I am too smart for this.
Why am I here?
Are promises that women make stronger or more binding?
I think it is time for my priorities to change,
I bet you believe that I am going to die first.
Long wait, bro!

Things That Make My Simple Soul Glad

Camping near a stream in midsummer

Putting my lawn chair in the shallow part of a stream in the sunlight

A clean house on Saturday morning and nothing to do Sunday morning

The smell of fabric softener in my fresh laundry and clean sheets

The smell of spring rain in the meadow

Getting anything free

Cooking for other people

The ocean at sunrise and sunset

Bright crimson/purple sunsets anywhere

Homemade chocolate pie

Simple art by simple people

Being at family reunions and eating country food

Irish music, Italian music, gospel music, bluegrass music

Poetry from the heart not the mind

Good, hot coffee waiting on me in the morning

My grandchildren's smiles when they see me and their tears when I leave

Thinking of my father

Teaching someone something and witnessing the lights in their eyes

Puppies, kittens, cubs, kits, and babies of any kind

Fossils, quartz, plants

Funny stories that really happened

Stories from old mountain people

Fishing

Vegetables straight from the garden

Pasta of any kind

Good lemonade

Cooking

Talking with God

Daydreams and Thinking Back...

This is the most eclectic of my poetry. As you have figured out by now, I do not like rhyming verses that much. I prefer free verse, as it is how I think. Now mind you, there are some that rhyme in my conglomeration of words, but not many. This group of poems go from one end of the spectrum to the other. There really isn't a pattern here, I suppose there will be some sign of my psychosis or my imagination, no matter. I go from love letters, to Santa Claus, to crazed dreams, onto the hallucinations while running a fever. I am not the type to scribble down every thought, but sometimes the words will not let me rest.

This grouping has no pattern, no reason or plan. Basically, these poems are what was left over. I wanted to add them for the sheer pleasure of publishing them because I can! If you were to know me, you would totally understand my being, my drive, and my convictions. I am a simple person who loves to entertain and to talk to people. I have things to say.

In the Search for Peace

I have attended little mountain churches
sparsely—filled with coal miners' widows and wiggly children,
cathedrals with spirals of concrete or wood
vases of flowers and sacred statuary
rows of seats of saddened people.
Stained glass filters the sins of outside
while I looked for peace,
I was left wanting
needing softness of soul
I turned to the outside to heal my inside.
In the calming effect of the forest
I found a large stone altar
the tallest tree is my steeple
my forest my cathedral,
the lace pine canopy is my painted ceiling
sunbeams that slip through the pine boughs
like hovering angel wings in the sunlight,
living color around me is my stained glass.

The message is so clear and uplifting
this is where God abides,
there are no locked doors here
the Holy Spirit is the caretaker
if I doze in quiet serenity
I have not missed the important message
as it resounds all around me.
The sweet sacred music of the breeze
blows through the trees, grasses, and laurel
as they sway to the sound of the chorus
I am at home here.
I found my new church
and at last I found peace
I found God.

An Ancient Meadow
(from a vision during illness)

I stood in a forgotten meadow

in view of a swift-moving creek,

I closed my eyes and quickly drifted to a time when

there was not a gate, or road, nor bridge.

I could smell the campfires of the people

hear the playing of the children and the barking of dogs,

there is great laughter and storytelling by the elders.

I hear the distant running of elk through the thick laurel,

the hawk screeches to his mate as he flies upward

blocking the sun with his wings as he gathers warmth,

this is a good time to be alive.

Drums sing of happiness and honor

a ceremony of bravery for the young men

rites of passage, a celebration for the whole tribe

I know them, I know their faces, I know their wigwams.

I take a deep breath and open my eyes

they fill with tears as I am back here

in the tall yellow grass of the meadow,

this forgotten place

that holds their bones so tenderly

no trace of campfires, no wigwams, the earth unscarred.

slowly I scan the visage once more

I leave and lock the gate behind me.

Always Together as a Song

And when the noise stops, and the world slows down

We will still have each other's melody.

Our souls are so like that of a beautifully made instrument,

Our hearts beat at the same time, with the same rhythm and become music,

We often finish each other's words as already known verses

My harp has many strings

You know my songs.

Time and space may separate us physically

But we will always be together like notes written in our rhapsody,

And when our world stops and the noise of life silences

We will continue singing our song.

In My Dreams
(St. Patrick's Day)

I dream of green mountains that are not my own,

Why do I see whitewashed cottages and neatly thatched roofs

with grey smoke rising from stone chimneys?

Even the sheep running on the green are familiar,

they run together like flocks of birds

and knowing like shamrocks and heather in the wind.

Why do I dream of ancient stone churches left in ruin

and hear a soprano voice sing hauntingly through the dark forests?

Am I thinking of another time in another life?

Could I be visiting my ancestors' memories or mine?

I have the Irish blood runnin' in my veins,

flowing strong like the song of an Innisfree fiddle,

it seems my feet have walked upon the cobblestones of a small town.

My hands long for the combing of the wool and fingers on the thread

I want to feel the spinning of the wheel turning as I did once long ago

and hear the rhythm of the foot pedal.

In Just One Night
(an analyst's playground)

Where are you taking me?

Why can't I move?

I'm alive

I can't talk

I feel strange.

Who are those other people,

where'd they come from?

Why are they looking at me that way?

Are you taking me to a hospital?

why are those lights flashing?

I am naked

walking down the hall

many rooms full of people.

Am I late for class?

Where's my locker?

I've got to find my clothes.

That greasy man is walking toward me,

he grabs a hand full of hair

jerking my head backward.

There's a knife in my hand,

I gut him like a fish and walk away.

Must get the blood off of me

where are the showers?

I am now at the house where I was born

there are other rooms behind the walls

we never knew they were there.

A room with pretty furniture

and bright windows with frilly eyelash curtains,

a table with fragile glass figurines

blinding sunlight pushing through the dim room

revealing more rooms on down the hallway.
I'm in my jeans, my favorite jeans with deep pockets
there are shiny dimes and quarters on the floor,
walking on I find gold jewelry scattered about like leaves.
I gather what I can and put them in my pockets
my old music teacher is playing Chopin,
snarling her too red lips at the frozen keys.
The house is flooding with rushing water
I swim between rooms and hallways
the water is growing past nose high,
I try to push out a window with my feet
but the window is locked and airtight.
My lungs burning and wanting me to gasp
I take one last breath full of warm water.
I wake setting up in the bed taking in the blessed air,
my heart beats as if I had been running
my husband turns his pillow and rolls over.

Is There a Question About Most Women?

Wanna know why most women are the strong ones?

Maybe we are closer to the Creator

After all, we do create life inside of us.

Are our men jealous? Dang skippy they are.

We are the nesting half of the pair,

We have a sense of survival that is all about our chicks

We would die for our chicks.

Our roosters are not first on the priorities list

That's no surprise, is it?

We get jobs that are unfairly ours, we get them done.

No need to squawk or whine, we just do it.

Roosters may come and go in our lives

We need to be cherished, honored, and loved

by one Rooster at a time.

It is She

It is She
that has given birth
makes things right
prepares the nourishment to please
keeps the clothes they wear clean
tends the house they live in
remembers birthdays, addresses and doctor appointments
kisses boo-boo magically taking the pain away
makes smiley face cupcakes for the bake sale
and gooey macaroni and cheese for church suppers
radiates patience and loyalty
inherited wisdom of the ages
emits love from all corners of her being
looks in the mirror and traces new lines
tears up at the raising of the flag
graduations, weddings and at funerals
she is left alone a lot, but she does not cry for that
she ages gracefully and dies the same way
her daughters will carry on
they become "She"

Life as a Chicken Salad

Life can be compared to a recipe.
Take chicken salad,
boil or bake the chicken
until "fork tender,"
then let it cool off,
it is pulled into small pieces
add an even mix of sweet and spicy things
to enhance the flavor
and mayonnaise, friends, to smooth it out.
Salt and pepper, yin and yang.
Sometimes a simple human cannot stand alone,
it gets too hot or it gets too cold
we need help with the recipe,
adding the spice of life
needing to smooth life out,
so we can belong to the salad
according to taste.

Queen of the Egypt, Daughter of Isis

I was young, chosen by a new pharaoh, a fulfilled destiny

I am a goddess, draped in flowing silk, Egyptian linen, my sandals are soft.

We rule together, our thrones side by side, golden with crook and flail.

We are worshiped, Horus and Isis. Every wish made real.

We hunt together, eat the fruit from our arbors, as we sacrifice to Geb,

servants wait, water poured from golden ornate vessels,

wine sweet and dark, figs and pomegranates prepared for my table.

Chariots polished for our horses, the royal blood of the desert,

our falcons, like Horus, wait for the hunt.

My children learn mathematics, the scholars and scribes attend them daily,

the royal family worships before Rah at sunrise, as we are the messengers of all the gods.

My tomb is grander than any other, my treasure for the afterlife is collected.

I will be honored by the gods in the grandest of fashion, fitting for my position.

I remember the day I closed my eyes to see the earth light no more.

Osiris, the great lord of death comes, husband and children, servants and slaves mourn,

the priests prepared my body, with such honor and respect for their goddess.

My body is cut in preparation, parts removed and in their sted, sweet herbs and spices are placed,

my body bathed in perfumed oils. I was pampered in death, as I was in life.

The urns that hold parts of me, rest beside my tomb,

my treasure rooms are rich, my adornment is richer.

My body is oiled and wrapped in the finest linen, dressed in gold threads woven by the gods,

my necklace of gold, rubies, and brilliant sapphires lay on my chest as my gold scarab

I am not asleep, I have been resting three thousand years.

I have been found, curious men have entered my sacred place,

white gloves and lights, they move me to another temple, it is acceptable.

People still come to worship me. My earth body is different, my soul is beautiful.

I see my home again. Egypt is the same.

The Nile still floods in spring, the fishermen still in their boats

throwing their nets like bones, the crocodiles still wait,

the reeds still dance to the music of the desert,

my sands still move with the impatient winds,

but the people no longer make mud bricks to bake in the sun for my family's tombs.

Why are the colors gone that once decorated our halls?

Our great pyramids were once red, the sphinx was gold.

Do the bright color and the bees leave the blossom?

Where are the caravans loaded with spices and silks?

The charioteers do not race, where are my priests, my scribes, my handmaidens?

They were to be with me after all this time.

Sahu gives me power. Anubis speaks as he shows the way after death.

Sail toward the sun, it is time. I am content.

I will leave this earthly plane, ride the golden barge across the sky,

climb the golden stair in search of my peace.

The Crossroads

I have been warned about the crossroads,
devil and angel wait to deal,
no advice or suggestions
just an intersection of two roads
void of anything interesting,
no one physically there to help and encourage.
This is not a one-time event
it can happen numerous times in one's life
and may never happen in others,
the only thing that you take with you
is the knowledge of it's not where you have been
but where you are going.
The choice,
the right path
the wrong path,
is for you only.

Sybil by the Sea
(Irish Ballad)

Sybil was a fair young maid she lived by the edge of the sea
Where she waited for handsome young Shawn,
Her husband to be, O her husband to be.

Young Shawn was a whaler gone for quite a while,
Sybil was a lady's maid
And pregnant with his child, O pregnant with his child.

The lady that she worked for had no children of her own
Her husband died long ago,
Leaving her all alone, O leaving her all alone.

Sybil lived at the big house, a small room in the back
But she would have her cottage dear
As soon as her Shawn got back, O as soon as her Shawn got back.

Sybil knew that cold night her lover's ship went down
by morning light, the news had spread
To everyone in the town, O everyone in the town.

Sybil could not show her face she couldn't bear the shame
She knew her baby would be marked,
Born without a name, O born without a name.

The lady watched 'ore Sybil as the midwives came and went
She knew poor Sybil's heart was broke
She knew her life was spent; O she knew her life was spent.

Sybil held the darling child and kissed the dear good-bye
Then gave her to the lady
as she closed her eyes and died, O she closed her eyes and died.

The lady raised the little girl as if she were her own
She had the pretty face of Sybil
and red hair just like Shawn, O red hair just like Shawn.

The lady and the little girl were as happy as could be
But little Sybil only smiled
While walking by the sea, O walking by the sea.

Sybil was a fair young maid who lived by the edge of the sea
Where she walks and waits
For handsome young Shawn,
her husband to be, O her husband to be.

The Most Torturous Night

Lying in bed trying to sleep
Santa won't come if we try to peep.
I've tossed, I've twisted and turned
Can't wait till morning for that day I've yearned.
My heart is beating hard in my chest
Knowing it's Christmas will not let me rest,
I wonder if I'll hear Santa up on the roof?
Wish I had a camera and I'd have my proof.
I have my new pajama's on, they're ok I guess
By the time I get up they'll be a wrinkled mess.
Does anyone have sympathy for kids at Christmas time?
Nobody knows the worry we have on our minds.
My brothers want bicycles and games of every kind
My sisters must have new clothes and shoes under the tree to find
I just want a pony with a long tail and mane so white,
We can keep him in the basement the space is just right.

And our yard has plenty of grass for him to eat when he gets hungry,
I could ride him to school on the days that mom does laundry.
I'm sure Santa got my letter, but he didn't let me know
I can see from my window it's beginning to snow!
Mom read the poem that we all love to hear,
She read it in our bedroom on Christmas Eve each year.
I am getting sleepy now and can hardly open my eyes
It has been a long day with candy, cakes, and pies,
I've played with cousins until I couldn't play anymore
I've just got to rest my eyes for just a minute or more
I'm not so nervous now, it will all be all right.
"Merry Christmas to all, and to all a good night!"
It thrilled my heart to hear.
She read it in our bedroom on Christmas Eve each year.

'Twas the Day After Christmas

'Twas the day after Christmas and back at the pole,
Santa was resting; the night took its toll.
The reindeer were brushed, watered, and fed
the Elves all ate breakfast and jumped into bed.
The sled's been washed, waxed, and dried
and put into storage for next year's ride.
Mamma Claus sings, and she finishes her chores
she bakes, she washes, amidst all the snores.
Seems for Mamma Claus the work never ends
when she gets one job finished, there is something to mend.
Santa's suit is now hanging to dry
his long johns and mittens are hanging nearby,
Mamma Claus has the morning to cook up his supper
the fragrance of ham, bread, and yams is a great "waker-upper."
This evening will be for their year's end office party
all the elves and Santa will feast long and hardy,
prizes awarded and presents exchanged with great applause
this is the best night of the year for Santa Claus.

*Tomorrow will begin the start of his new year
but tonight, they celebrate, and it ends with a cheer!
Mamma and Santa are alone finally at last,
comparing this party with the ones of the past.
Santa smiles at Mamma and gives her a kiss,
and says to her, "Thank you, darling, for all of this,
I could not have done it, if it were not for you!"
Mamma just smiles, she knows it is true,
she kisses her sweet Santa on top of his head
then they walk hand in hand upstairs to bed.*

My Older Days...

Now that I am older, on my journey to get here, I think I have become more aware. Does it come with age? Perhaps it's getting toward the last part of my life, I want to remember everything. I don't believe I was this observant even just a few years ago. So, I can blame my old age with this grouping of my poetry. I also added another Christmas poem in here just for no real reason, it really didn't fit anywhere else. I wanted this "Older Days" section for last, guess that choice speaks for itself. But, still I remember.

The poems here are about getting older, and one, "Miss Ruth is Missing," is for a couple of special friends who had Alzheimer's Disease. We will all suffer the loss of friends, family, and other things. Read and understand that I don't want to be morbid, just real. I also want to portray my wanting to be a good role model and to hang on to life with everything I have left. It's no secret that I always felt that one should stay active and busy if they can, all the way to the end. I hope when people think of me after I am gone, they will think kindly of me and know in their hearts that I meant well.

Going "gently into that good night" is not the plan. You can bet that I will go down scratching and fighting all the way. I hope you can relate.

What About the Word "OLD"?

*I like to think of the word "Old" as not a tag
on someone or something,
but a measure of survival and knowledge,
a keeper, something that has been proven.
Old just means not so new,
like an old coin, or a masterpiece hanging in a museum.
People like to have old coins or an antiquated piece of art.
They have become valuable.
A price? Yes, paid with the ages of pain, tears,
and every emotion in between.
Old is wise and needful at a time such as this, but then again
Old has seen times like this too.
Old is still around.
The shine on "new" quickly tarnishes
and hopefully will gain a fine patina
such as Old has acquired
before silently slipping away.*

Evolution, Revolution, and Change

I look at my mother with different eyes
seeing things that have changed in the passing of time,
as my mother's appearance.
I do not see her as an old being, just older
I know her body has changed,
I see changes in mine,
she is shorter and moves slower
her skin is transparent as cellophane,
the once tanned smooth hands that strongly opened doors
now lightly tremble with blue veins.
She doesn't scold now but listens to me
the woman who did not need anyone, is taking medication
her house is a little dusty, but tidy
it was not that tidy when we were all together.
Her house is strangely quiet and smells of her perfume,
dad is gone and so are all their old friends
she still grieves the loss
nothing is the same.
Loneliness turns the television on for noise
I find myself sounding like her
I look in the mirror and trace the lines
that lead to a pattern I recognize.

Me in the Mirror

Is my reflection that I see in my mirror stuck deep inside the glass?

Somewhere past the surface where all my images have gone from times of beauty past,

hidden submerged in fathoms deep with all my imperfections and disappointments.

Looking into the glass for answers or self-assurance.

Will the glass images tell their secrets to some stranger when I am through?

The glass was my only friend that would lie sweetly one moment,

and be painfully truthful in another,

it was always there somewhere for me to cast a glance,

searching for familiarity and false security in reverse,

a history of my face and body encased in some other shiny cold hard place.

I would stop if I could but there is so much of me in there already.

Maybe it is the mirror instead of my eyes that is a window to my soul,

I want to be like Alice and walk through to see what is on the other side.

Perhaps I would want to stay there and not come out on this end.

If I were blind through age or accident would the mirror let me in?

If I grow deaf would I remember how it spoke to me of gray hairs and lines?

What if I become mute, would it still have the ability to listen to my silenced words?

Would the need for it be as great as it once was on this side of it?

I will continue to clean the mirror of its fingerprints and toothbrush spray,

careful not to break it so that I will not ooze out of the cracks.

At the Hour of His Death

His daughter smoothed his hair with her hand,
the doctor said the time of death was near.
His breathing was labored
he had slept for two days,
suddenly his breath is regular
and his face has softened.
He opens his eyes and looks over to the corner,
"You're here," he whispers.
The daughter says, "yes dad, I am here."
"No, not you, it's your uncle Charlie!
I never thought I would see him again
hello brother, hey, you brought mom,
she looks beautiful
and little sister Anna came too!"
The daughter looks to the bare corner,
she stands helplessly
"Can't you see them, honey?"
"They look so wonderful!"
The daughter holds his hands strongly,
as he takes one last deep breath
closes his eyes and with a calm smile
his glad heart stops.

Miss Ruth is Missing

Rocking on her front porch
Miss Ruth hums a lullaby to her cradled lifelike doll
she has decided not to be in today
she sees her children playing there in the yard
unaware of time, being in the evening of her life
her sun is setting, but she lives in her morning
with her babies

Sam, has been gone for years
still, she waits for him to come home for supper
do not look for Miss Ruth and do not feel sad
she is in the place that she loved best
a safe place with no surprises, no strangers
she doesn't love the "now" like she loves "then"
it's a familiar place

She waited for something she was not sure of
each day seemed like the one before
the gate and the doors are locked
She became a prisoner in her own house
She just decided to let go and dream.
What a good day to be on the porch
waiting for Sam.

He Died

What will I do now?

The service is over and everyone has gone home

all the plants have been distributed to family members that wanted them

the fried chicken, rolls, and chocolate cake are put up

Sissy wanted to stay with me for a few days

to see if I was going to commit suicide or something stupid like that.

my husband died, I did not have a stroke or brain damage

why now do they think I cannot continue with my life

without their guidance or their paid-for-wisdom?

Sissy packed up and left this morning after I cooked breakfast

she left me all teary-eyed, a sink full of dishes and sheets to change

I went to the mailbox

just a bundle of sympathy cards,

and a sales flyer from the Mall

I never shopped there, why do they want me now?

do they cater to widows?

how did they know?

his closet is full of his clothes and the essence of him

I hold one of his suits to my face and breathe deep so I will remember

The smell of his aftershave, cedar and him

on the chest of drawers are his billfold, loose change and half-eaten roll of Rolaids

the extra set of car keys, a picture of us, and dust

the bed where we slept has two pillows. His side has the alarm clock

death happened too fast for us

we had no warning

we were going to grow old together, now what?

My Time

I thought about reaching my old age since I was very young.

I have always feared the moment of death,

The dreaded event of closing my eyes for the last time.

When I was young, I would cry because I had to die

And my mom would try to comfort me as best she could.

She is older now and she too fears death.

Now it is my time to comfort her. To ease her fears as she once did mine.

But how do I do that? I am still afraid to die.

I love being on this side of the flower bed. I still want to do so many things.

Does it matter if we die scratching and screaming, not wanting to go?

Are we going to be graded on our performance?

Is this the time to worry about dignity? I don't think so.

Only you pass into the unknown.

I compare it to birth. It is all about YOU, passing into the unknown.

Will we come into another place crying and naked? I have heard that babies are made to forget about heaven the minute they are born.

Will this happen to us as we travel through that long tunnel to the light? Are we going to forget life, the people we have known and loved, the things we knew?

I believe it was Confucius that said that the anticipation of death is worse than death its self.

I hope so.

Picky in My Old Age

I used to love winter.

youth can find fun in anything.

the older me desires sun's warmth.

I just want to look at snow from my window

or the scorched grass from my air-conditioned living room.

I don't want to be too hot, or too cold. That's my prerogative.

aching muscles and sinus pain are frequent flyers in the winter season

they sleep during the warmer seasons so my hay fever won't be too crowded.

arthritis moves in as adaptability moves out

noise in either season is bothersome. Lawn mowers, snow blowers and loud radios

sleeping seems to be a little more important, and a lot harder to attain

so is the uninvited light that peeps in through the curtains

seems when I get settled in just right…

the telephone rings, I get up, I loose that spot in my pillow that I worked so hard to find

the sheets get cool, the comfort leaves, the furnace kicks on

and after wondering if that stupid call could have waited until tomorrow

damn, I am about to pee again.

Renewal

If you concentrate real hard and try to listen,
you'll hear the voices singing through the pines.
A little old log cabin once stood right hear,
I can hear my grandma calling supper time.

Away 'bout over there was the meadow.
I'm sure the children played there all the time.
And where we stand it used to be the garden,
now taken over by the weed and vine.

I understand the family's coming back here,
they'll clean it up and make it look just fine.
Our family's love is going to be renewed here.
You'll hear the voices singing through the pines.

The old folks up in Heaven will be smiling,
after all these years they know it's 'bout time.
The laughter of the children in the meadow,
and the singing voices echo in the pines.

Building back the memories that we all loved,
renewing all the pride that we once shared.
The new ones being blessed from God above,
letting our singing voices fill the air.

The Retirement Cabin

They built the log cabin together

a restful place for saved dreams,

fishing and gardening together

alone in their quiet cove

every morning before the sunrise.

I passed the little cabin as I drove to work

alone, he would quietly sit in his kitchen drinking coffee

reading his morning paper by one small private light,

always blowing my car horn lightly to the satisfied stranger

I looked forward to seeing him there every morning through that kitchen window.

I wished my life was that predictable, calm, and simple

until that day when the signs were on the road before the curve,

"Slow Funeral, Thank you. Bennett Funeral Home"

the driveway full of shiny clean cars and people carrying foil covered food.

The cars are gone and the driveway is empty

Dampened morning news still waits in the plastic paper box,

as I drive past the little cabin is dark.

I don't blow my horn anymore

but I can't help looking over there

as I pass on my way to work,

he had his time and his season.

The Time Machine

How I love to visit
run with the children
school days
daddy holding my hand
my mother's laughter
school chums
first love
first kiss
high school plays
flirtations
invitations
graduations
my grandmother's wisdom
family suppers
Sundays, Christmas, birthdays, Easter
dances after the ballgames
holding each other close
those wonderful times
those wonderful places
I visit often
sitting here in my chair
before the fireplace
I take the time machine
to happy times and places I have known
any time.

The Puzzle of the Garden

Life can be complicated, it isn't easy learning the "Book,"

But a dream I had last night, made me have another look.

My dream showed me a garden all lush and full of green

The trees and vines were fruited full, the most beautiful I had ever seen.

I walked through the garden, the furrows long and straight,

Each plant was ready for harvest, it seemed they could not wait.

I know it was a hearty task to turn and cultivate.

Who was the keeper here? Who held the garden gate?

Who took the stones and made the wall?

Who planted all these lovely things, standing straight and tall?

Who fought the flood, the pests, and the drought?

Who planted and seeded and weeded throughout?

I know now the garden is my soul.

The victory of the garden depends on how I toil,

The stones that dull the plow you used to make the wall

Built strong and study, but not too tall.

Others must see the garden

They learn by how you seed,

I know the Master Gardener who sees our soul,

Will take care of all our needs.

Time to Think

I sit and wonder how I got this far.
I remember planning many things to do
before I got to where I am now,
but life got in the way.
School, marriage, children, jobs, PTA
little league, Girl Scouts, Boy Scouts
funerals, weddings, homecomings,
all seemed to happen at once
lingering on through my planning years.
Now, I sit and wonder where the time went.
My children are gone to plan their own lives,
my husband doesn't seem to worry about the time.
He never did worry about anything,
time was not an issue with him,
but it was I, who drove from here to there
sewed every stitch, cooked every morsel
washed every sock and dish in the house.
Now, I sit and wonder why I was chosen
to make this family my responsibility?
my blood…my sweat…my tears,
my years are all gone.
Things remembered by me only.
Now, that I have time.
I sit and wonder.

My Class Reunion

I went to my class reunion
to see my friends
from long ago
pictures of grandchildren
stories of lives
stories of success
packaged lies
presenting themselves
as in a grand ballet of life
turning
pirouetting properly
taking their bows
how'd they get so old
why haven't I aged as much as they
wondering why I am not like them
so settled with their lives
so successful and finished

fancy cars and mansions on a hill
living far away from here
guess I am just me
still trying to get by
in last year's clothes.
they traded emails
swearing devotion
exchanged phone numbers
lasting forever
forgotten by the time
they got into their shiny cars
drove away
into the sunset

About the Author

Born Appalachian and raised running the hills of McDowell County, West Virginia, Teresa Jewell went to school in War, West Virginia and became a hairdresser. She owned her own salon for approximately thirty years. While doing hair, Jewell was known to tell stories and recite poetry to her customers. She is a mother and a grandmother, and is married to a mountain man. Jewell went on to graduate with a M.S from Radford University. She now teaches Appalachian Literature and English at Southwest Virginia Community College. Her hobbies include drawing, painting, reading, writing, poetry, and bluegrass music.

www.ingramcontent.com/pod-product-compliance
Lightning Source LLC
Chambersburg PA
CBHW031403160426
43196CB00007B/871